Moon Tuition

YEAR 5 CLOZE TEST

www.moontuition.co.uk

Contents

T1. Prince of Mathematicians

Carl Friedrich Gauss (30 April 30 1777 – 23 February 1855) was a famous German mathematician. Gauss contributed to many areas of learning so sometimes Gauss is referred to as the "Prince of Mathematicians". Gauss is also _____ to be one of the three greatest mathematicians of all time.

As a child, Gauss was a_____, meaning he was very clever. When he was 3 years old, he told his father that he had _____ measured something on his complicated account. Gauss was correct. Gauss also taught _____ to read.

_____ Gauss was in primary school, his teacher once tried to keep the children busy, telling them to add up all the numbers from 1 to 100.

Gauss recognised he had fifty pairs of numbers when he added the first and last number in the_____, the second and second-last number in the series, and so on. For example: (1 + 100), (2 + 99), (3 + 98), . . . , and each pair has a sum of 101.

   50 pairs × 101 (the sum of each pair) = 5,050.

In_____ , to find the sum of all the numbers from 1 to N:

   $1 + 2 + 3 + 4 + ... + N = (1 + N)*N/2$

Although his family was poor and working class, Gauss' intellectual abilities _____ the attention of the Duke of Brunswick, who sent him to the university. At just 19 years of age, he constructed a hitherto , _____ regular seventeen-sided figure using only a ruler and compass, a major advance in this field since the time of Greek mathematics. Gauss also _____ that every positive integer is representable as a sum of at most three triangular numbers.

considered, attracted,   unknown, general , proved, series, When, himself, prodigy, incorrectly

A1. Prince of Mathematicians

Carl Friedrich Gauss (30 April 30 1777 – 23 February 1855) was a famous German mathematician. Gauss contributed to many areas of learning so sometimes Gauss is referred to as the "Prince of Mathematicians". Gauss is also **considered** to be one of the three greatest mathematicians of all time.

As a child, Gauss was a **prodigy**, meaning he was very clever. When he was 3 years old, he told his father that he had **incorrectly** measured something on his complicated account. Gauss was correct. Gauss also taught **himself** to read.

When Gauss was in primary school, his teacher once tried to keep the children busy, telling them to add up all the numbers from 1 to 100.

Gauss recognised he had fifty pairs of numbers when he added the first and last number in the **series**, the second and second-last number in the series, and so on. For example: (1 + 100), (2 + 99), (3 + 98), . . . , and each pair has a sum of 101.

50 pairs × 101 (the sum of each pair) = 5,050.

In **general**, to find the sum of all the numbers from 1 to N:

$$1 + 2 + 3 + 4 + \ldots + N = (1 + N)*N/2$$

Although his family was poor and working class, Gauss' intellectual abilities **attracted** the attention of the Duke of Brunswick, who sent him to the university. At just 19 years of age, he constructed a hitherto **unknown** regular seventeen-sided figure using only a ruler and compass, a major advance in this field since the time of Greek mathematics. Gauss also **proved** that every positive integer is representable as a sum of at most three triangular numbers.

T2. Standing upon the Shoulders of Giants

Isaac Newton was born on January 4, 1643 in a tiny village in Lincolnshire, England. His father, whose name was also Isaac Newton, was a farmer who died before Isaac Junior was born. Although comfortable _____, his father could not read or write.

At age 12, Newton attended The King's School, Grantham, where he was _____ the classics, but no science or mathematics. When he was 17, his mother stopped his schooling so that he could become a farmer. _____ for the future of science Newton found he had neither _____ nor liking for farming; his mother allowed him to return to school, where he finished as top student.

In June 1661, aged 18, Newton began studying for a law degree at Cambridge University's Trinity College, _____ money working as a personal servant to wealthier students. By the time he was a third-year student he was _____ a lot of his time studying mathematics and natural philosophy (today we call it physics). He was also very interested in alchemy, which we now categorize as a pseudoscience.

"Plato is my friend, Aristotle is my friend, but my greatest friend is_____ ."

"I do not know what I may appear to the world, but to myself I seem to have been only like a boy playing on the seashore, and _____ myself in now and then finding a smoother pebble or a prettier shell than ordinary, whilst the great ocean of truth lay all undiscovered before me."

 "If I have seen _____ than others, it is by standing upon the shoulders of giants."

"Genius is _____."

patience, further, diverting, spending truth, taught , earning, aptitude, Fortunately, financially

A2. Standing upon the Shoulders of Giants

Isaac Newton was born on January 4, 1643 in a tiny village in Lincolnshire, England. His father, whose name was also Isaac Newton, was a farmer who died before Isaac Junior was born. Although comfortable **financially**, his father could not read or write.

At age 12, Newton attended The King's School, Grantham, where he was **taught** the classics, but no science or mathematics. When he was 17, his mother stopped his schooling so that he could become a farmer. **Fortunately** for the future of science Newton found he had neither **aptitude** nor liking for farming; his mother allowed him to return to school, where he finished as top student.

In June 1661, aged 18, Newton began studying for a law degree at Cambridge University's Trinity College, **earning** money working as a personal servant to wealthier students. By the time he was a third-year student he was **spending** a lot of his time studying mathematics and natural philosophy (today we call it physics). He was also very interested in alchemy, which we now categorize as a pseudoscience.

"Plato is my friend, Aristotle is my friend, but my greatest friend is **truth**."

"I do not know what I may appear to the world, but to myself I seem to have been only like a boy playing on the seashore, and **diverting** myself in now and then finding a smoother pebble or a prettier shell than ordinary, whilst the great ocean of truth lay all undiscovered before me."

"If I have seen **further** than others, it is by standing upon the shoulders of giants."

Genius is **patience**.

T3. Is this the end for tailcoats at Eton College?

Simon Henderson greets me with an _____. Eton's new headmaster – at 39 the youngest ever – says he can't welcome me into his office because he hasn't got one yet.

It is not, however, a sign that he's _____ to find his feet at Britain's most famous public school, alma mater to 19 prime ministers, including the incumbent, and many others now at the pinnacle of public life.

Quite the _____ . Henderson is relocating the head's study from its traditional spot in a quiet corner of an ancient quad to a central new location where the 1,300 pupils mill about between lessons. "I want to be in the _____ of the passing traffic of boys," he tells me.

In a school where the boys still wear Victorian tailcoats and white dickey bows to lessons, their head is instead sporting what he calls "teacher casual" – a linen jacket and chino-like trousers. He dons a tie for the photographs but discards it _____ after.

Will he be extending that _____ to the 1,300 pupils? "Tradition is important here," he replies cautiously, "and the uniform is a physical connection with that tradition._____ , Eton hasn't survived since 1440 by relying on tradition_____. It has constantly reinvented itself." So is he hinting that something a little more 21st century might be on the cards?

"I'm not getting rid of the uniform this week," he replies with an expression that suggests "watch this_____ ". He has perfected the knack of embodying the spirit of change, without actually _____ anything concrete.

apology, space, promising, However, alone, privilege, middle   immediately, opposite, struggling

A3. Is this the end for tailcoats at Eton College?

Simon Henderson greets me with an **apology**. Eton's new headmaster – at 39 the youngest ever – says he can't welcome me into his office because he hasn't got one yet.

It is not, however, a sign that he's **struggling** to find his feet at Britain's most famous public school, alma mater to 19 prime ministers, including the incumbent, and many others now at the pinnacle of public life.

Quite the **opposite**. Henderson is relocating the head's study from its traditional spot in a quiet corner of an ancient quad to a central new location where the 1,300 pupils mill about between lessons. "I want to be in the **middle** of the passing traffic of boys," he tells me.

In a school where the boys still wear Victorian tailcoats and white dickey bows to lessons, their head is instead sporting what he calls "teacher casual" – a linen jacket and chino-like trousers. He dons a tie for the photographs but discards it **immediately** after.

Will he be extending that **privilege** to the 1,300 pupils? "Tradition is important here," he replies cautiously, "and the uniform is a physical connection with that tradition. **However**, Eton hasn't survived since 1440 by relying on tradition **alone**. It has constantly reinvented itself." So is he hinting that something a little more 21st century might be on the cards?

"I'm not getting rid of the uniform this week," he replies with an expression that suggests "watch this **space**". He has perfected the knack of embodying the spirit of change, without actually **promising** anything concrete.

T4. Malala Yousafzai wins Oxford university place

Five years ago, the Taliban _____ Malala Yousafzai in the head for advocating the right of girls to be educated. Now she has _____ a place at Lady Margaret Hall, University of Oxford, to study philosophy, politics and economics, or PPE.

The 20-year-old Nobel peace prize winner _____ a screenshot of the confirmation and said: "So excited to go to Oxford!! Well done to all A-level students – the hardest year. Best wishes for life ahead!"

Yousafzai comes from the Swat valley, an area in north-west Pakistan which has periodically _____ girls from attending school. When the Taliban were driven out of the region in 2012, Yousafzai _____ up her campaign for girls to be allowed to go to school.

Her persistence and the growing prominence of her activism – she had _____ anonymously for BBC Urdu when she was just 11 in 2009 – prompted the Taliban to hold a meeting in 2012 at which they unanimously agreed to _____ her.

A few months later, a Taliban gunman shot the schoolgirl as she _____ home after an exam. In a coma for eight days, Yousafzai was _____ first in Pakistan then sent to the UK, to the Queen Elizabeth hospital in Birmingham, for treatment.

Earlier this year, Yousafzai revealed she had _____ an offer from Oxford, which was conditional on achieving three As at A-level. Yousafzai took A-levels in history, maths, religious studies and geography.

Shot received returned treated blogged stepped murder banned won tweeted

A4. Malala Yousafzai wins Oxford university place

Five years ago, the Taliban **shot** Malala Yousafzai in the head for advocating the right of girls to be educated. Now she has **won** a place at Lady Margaret Hall, University of Oxford, to study philosophy, politics and economics, or PPE.

The 20-year-old Nobel peace prize winner **tweeted** a screenshot of the confirmation and said: "So excited to go to Oxford!! Well done to all A-level students – the hardest year. Best wishes for life ahead!"

Yousafzai comes from the Swat valley, an area in north-west Pakistan which has periodically **banned** girls from attending school. When the Taliban were driven out of the region in 2012, Yousafzai **stepped** up her campaign for girls to be allowed to go to school.

Her persistence and the growing prominence of her activism – she had **blogged** anonymously for BBC Urdu when she was just 11 in 2009 – prompted the Taliban to hold a meeting in 2012 at which they unanimously agreed to **murder** her.

A few months later, a Taliban gunman shot the schoolgirl as she **returned** home after an exam. In a coma for eight days, Yousafzai was **treated** first in Pakistan then sent to the UK, to the Queen Elizabeth hospital in Birmingham, for treatment.

Earlier this year, Yousafzai revealed she had **received** an offer from Oxford, which was conditional on achieving three As at A-level. Yousafzai took A-levels in history, maths, religious studies and geography.

T5. Big Issue seller wins 'dream' place at Cambridge University

A former Big Issue seller has gone from _____ on the streets to studying English Literature at Cambridge University.

Geoff Edwards, 52, _____ up in Liverpool and left school with two O-levels, he then worked as a field labourer before moving to Cambridge in search of more steady employment.

He spent years living in squats and on the streets of the River Cam city, spending most of his adult life homeless, while also _____ from depression.

Mr Edwards, who had a _____ for reading from an early age, then began selling the Big Issue and he turned his life _____ when he attended an open day at Cambridge Regional College (CRC).

"I came to Cambridge from Liverpool to do field work, but the work dried up. I was homeless for a long time after that and I was isolated and getting _____. Eventually I started selling the Big Issue on the streets of Cambridge which helped and gave me back a bit of self-respect," he said.

"I knew I was in a rut and I decided to do something _____ with my life. I thought about how to address it and decided education was the way so I went to an open day at Cambridge Regional College. I wanted to get the _____ to do English at university but I'd had a long time out of education and I only had Maths and English O levels, so I needed to do a gateway course. "

He gained _____ in an Access to Higher Education course, which gave him the qualifications needed to apply to one of the world's most _____ universities.

distinctions prestigious qualifications suffering passion different around anxious grew living

A5. Big Issue seller wins 'dream' place at Cambridge University

A former Big Issue seller has gone from **living** on the streets to studying English Literature at Cambridge University.

Geoff Edwards, 52, **grew** up in Liverpool and left school with two O-levels, he then worked as a field labourer before moving to Cambridge in search of more steady employment.

He spent years living in squats and on the streets of the River Cam city, spending most of his adult life homeless, while also **suffering** from depression.

Mr Edwards, who had a **passion** for reading from an early age, then began selling the Big Issue and he turned his life **around** when he attended an open day at Cambridge Regional College (CRC).

"I came to Cambridge from Liverpool to do field work, but the work dried up. I was homeless for a long time after that and I was isolated and getting **anxious**. Eventually I started selling the Big Issue on the streets of Cambridge which helped and gave me back a bit of self-respect," he said.

"I knew I was in a rut and I decided to do something **different** with my life. I thought about how to address it and decided education was the way so I went to an open day at Cambridge Regional College. I wanted to get the **qualifications** to do English at university but I'd had a long time out of education and I only had Maths and English O levels, so I needed to do a gateway course. "

He gained **distinctions** in an Access to Higher Education course, which gave him the qualifications needed to apply to one of the world's most **prestigious** universities.

T6. Sal Khan: the man who started a revolution

Sal Khan has a _____ mission: a free, world-class education for anyone, anywhere. Naturally, people think he's crazy. The _____ part is not the "world-class education" part, because plenty of people want that. And it's not even the "for anyone, anywhere" part. It's the "free" part.

Crazy or not, it's an idea that has _____ attention from Downing Street to Washington DC. And like a lot of crazy ideas, it started by _____.

Khan – working as a financial analyst in 2004 after earning degrees from MIT and an MBA from Harvard – started _____ tutoring his cousin, Nadia, in Louisiana, who was struggling with maths. "Then the rest of the family heard there was free tutoring," he says, and more relatives started taking part. The _____ got too much – until a friend suggested he could film the tutorials, post them on YouTube and let the family members view them whenever they chose.

"YouTube? YouTube was for cats playing the piano, not serious mathematics," Khan recalls thinking. "I got over the idea that it wasn't my idea and _____ to give it a shot."

Since 2009, Khan has _____ himself full-time to his Khan Academy, a tutoring, mentoring and testing educational website at khanacademy.org that offers its content free to anyone with internet access willing to work through its exercises and pithy videos, the majority _____ by Khan himself.

Khan is no fan of traditional education, which he derides as "lecture, homework, lecture, homework". "The _____ problem is that the process is broken," he tells his LSE audience, to nods of approval. "We identify the gaps [in children's knowledge], then we ignore them."

simple real devoted narrated demands decided remotely attracted accident craziest

A6. Sal Khan: the man who started a revolution

Sal Khan has a **simple** mission: a free, world-class education for anyone, anywhere. Naturally, people think he's crazy. The **craziest** part is not the "world-class education" part, because plenty of people want that. And it's not even the "for anyone, anywhere" part. It's the "free" part.

Crazy or not, it's an idea that has **attracted** attention from Downing Street to Washington DC. And like a lot of crazy ideas, it started by **accident**.

Khan – working as a financial analyst in 2004 after earning degrees from MIT and an MBA from Harvard – started **remotely** tutoring his cousin, Nadia, in Louisiana, who was struggling with maths. "Then the rest of the family heard there was free tutoring," he says, and more relatives started taking part. The **demands** got too much – until a friend suggested he could film the tutorials, post them on YouTube and let the family members view them whenever they chose.

"YouTube? YouTube was for cats playing the piano, not serious mathematics," Khan recalls thinking. "I got over the idea that it wasn't my idea and **decided** to give it a shot."

Since 2009, Khan has **devoted** himself full-time to his Khan Academy, a tutoring, mentoring and testing educational website at khanacademy.org that offers its content free to anyone with internet access willing to work through its exercises and pithy videos, the majority **narrated** by Khan himself.

Khan is no fan of traditional education, which he derides as "lecture, homework, lecture, homework". "The **real** problem is that the process is broken," he tells his LSE audience, to nods of approval. "We identify the gaps [in children's knowledge], then we ignore them."

T7. Rockstar Scientist

_____ he was a scientist who used to be a rockstar, now he's a rockstar scientist. So successful have his TV programmes become that Professor Brian Cox is more in the limelight now than he _____ was as a member of the chart-topping D:Ream in the Nineties. "I was playing keyboard so I was _____ at the back," he tells me, when we meet to discuss Human Universe, his cosmology series starting tonight on BBC Two.

Prof Cox is returning to our screens to ask _____ questions about our existence. Why are we here? How did the universe make us? What made the universe? The series is, he says, a love letter to the human race. "During the shooting I realised that we are rare and _____ valuable and quite remarkable and worth celebrating." In the first programme, he takes us on a fast-track journey from monkey to the space station.

Tall but slight, Prof Cox is a youthful 46, _____ his trademark fringe is beginning to grey. He was born in Greater Manchester to parents who worked in a bank and was privately educated at Hulme Grammar School in the Eighties. He _____ in physics but got a D in his maths A-level (he was "more interested in New Order and the Smiths"). _____, he lives in London with his wife, the American television presenter Gia Milinovich, their five-year-old son and her son from a previous relationship.

Prof Cox is, before anything else, a scientist and still does research and gives an annual lecture course. "I'm a Manchester academic. I don't do TV _____ I want a career in the media. Science is very important. It's undervalued and underinvested in and it's a force for extreme good in education, in society and economically. So there's a polemical element to _____ I want to do, but I enjoy making these films. I like learning curves and it's brilliant to work with creative people."

Once what because Today though excelled therefore always profound ever

A7. Rockstar Scientist

Once he was a scientist who used to be a rockstar, now he's a rockstar scientist. So successful have his TV programmes become that Professor Brian Cox is more in the limelight now than he **ever** was as a member of the chart-topping D:Ream in the Nineties. "I was playing keyboard so I was **always** at the back," he tells me, when we meet to discuss Human Universe, his cosmology series starting tonight on BBC Two.

Prof Cox is returning to our screens to ask **profound** questions about our existence. Why are we here? How did the universe make us? What made the universe? The series is, he says, a love letter to the human race. "During the shooting I realised that we are rare and **therefore** valuable and quite remarkable and worth celebrating." In the first programme, he takes us on a fast-track journey from monkey to the space station.

Tall but slight, Prof Cox is a youthful 46, **though** his trademark fringe is beginning to grey. He was born in Greater Manchester to parents who worked in a bank and was privately educated at Hulme Grammar School in the Eighties. He **excelled** in physics but got a D in his maths A-level (he was "more interested in New Order and the Smiths"). **Today**, he lives in London with his wife, the American television presenter Gia Milinovich, their five-year-old son and her son from a previous relationship.

Prof Cox is, before anything else, a scientist and still does research and gives an annual lecture course. "I'm a Manchester academic. I don't do TV **because** I want a career in the media. Science is very important. It's undervalued and underinvested in and it's a force for extreme good in education, in society and economically. So there's a polemical element to **what** I want to do, but I enjoy making these films. I like learning curves and it's brilliant to work with creative people."

T9. I Wandered Lonely as a Cloud

BY WILLIAM WORDSWORTH

I wandered _____ as a cloud

That floats on high o'er vales and hills,

When all at once I saw a _____,

A host, of golden daffodils;

Beside the lake, _____ the trees,

Fluttering and dancing in the breeze.

Continuous as the stars that shine

And _____ on the milky way,

They stretched in never-ending _____

Along the margin of a bay:

Ten thousand saw I at a glance,

Tossing their heads in sprightly _____.

The waves beside them danced; but they

Out-did the _____ waves in glee:

A poet could not but be gay,

In such a jocund company:

I gazed—and gazed—but little thought

What wealth the show to me had _____:

For oft, when on my couch I lie

In vacant or in pensive _____,

They flash upon that inward eye

Which is the bliss of solitude;

And then my heart with pleasure fills,

And dances with the _____.

daffodils mood brought sparkling dance lonely line crowd twinkle beneath

A9. I Wandered Lonely as a Cloud

BY WILLIAM WORDSWORTH

I wandered **lonely** as a cloud

That floats on high o'er vales and hills,

When all at once I saw a **crowd**,

A host, of golden daffodils;

Beside the lake, **beneath** the trees,

Fluttering and dancing in the breeze.

Continuous as the stars that shine

And **twinkle** on the milky way,

They stretched in never-ending **line**

Along the margin of a bay:

Ten thousand saw I at a glance,

Tossing their heads in sprightly **dance**.

The waves beside them danced; but they

Out-did the **sparkling** waves in glee:

A poet could not but be gay,

In such a jocund company:

I gazed—and gazed—but little thought

What wealth the show to me had **brought**:

For oft, when on my couch I lie

In vacant or in pensive **mood**,

They flash upon that inward eye

Which is the bliss of solitude;

And then my heart with pleasure fills,

And dances with the **daffodils**.

T10. Little Red Riding Hood and the Wolf

By Roald Dahl

As soon as Wolf began to feel

That he would like a decent _____,

He went and knocked on Grandma's door.

When Grandma opened it, she saw

The _____ white teeth, the horrid grin,

And Wolfie said, 'May I come in?'

Poor Grandmamma was terrified,

'He's going to eat me up!' she_____.

And she was absolutely right.

He ate her up in one big bite.

But Grandmamma was small and tough,

And Wolfie wailed, 'That's not _____!

'I haven't yet begun to feel

'That I have had a decent meal!'

He ran around the kitchen yelping,

'I've got to have another _____!'

Then added with a frightful leer,

'I'm _____ going to wait right here

'Till Little Miss Red Riding Hood

'Comes home from walking in the_____ .'

He quickly put on Grandma's clothes,

(Of course he hadn't eaten those.)

He _____ himself in coat and hat.

He put on shoes and after that

He even _____ and curled his hair,

Then sat himself in Grandma's _____.

In came the little girl in red.

chair brushed dressed wood therefore helping enough meal cried sharp

A10. Little Red Riding Hood and the Wolf

By Roald Dahl

As soon as Wolf began to feel

That he would like a decent **meal**,

He went and knocked on Grandma's door.

When Grandma opened it, she saw

The **sharp** white teeth, the horrid grin,

And Wolfie said, 'May I come in?'

Poor Grandmamma was terrified,

'He's going to eat me up!' she **cried**.

And she was absolutely right.

He ate her up in one big bite.

But Grandmamma was small and tough,

And Wolfie wailed, 'That's not **enough**!

'I haven't yet begun to feel

'That I have had a decent meal!'

He ran around the kitchen yelping,

'I've got to have another **helping**!'

Then added with a frightful leer,

'I'm **therefore** going to wait right here

'Till Little Miss Red Riding Hood

'Comes home from walking in the **wood**.'

He quickly put on Grandma's clothes,

(Of course he hadn't eaten those.)

He **dressed** himself in coat and hat.

He put on shoes and after that

He even **brushed** and curled his hair,

Then sat himself in Grandma's **chair**.

In came the little girl in red.

Printed in Great Britain
by Amazon